GHAZAL GAMES

GHAZAL GAMES

POEMS

ROGER SEDARAT

OHIO UNIVERSITY PRESS
ATHENS, OHIO

Ohio University Press, Athens, Ohio 45701
ohioswallow.com

To obtain permission to quote, reprint, or otherwise reproduce or distribute material
from Ohio University Press publications, please contact our rights and permissions
department at (740) 593-1154 or (740) 593-4536 (fax).

Printed in the United States of America
Ohio University Press books are printed on acid-free paper ⊚ ™

20 19 18 17 16 15 14 13 12 11   5 4 3 2 1

Library of Congress Cataloging-in-Publication Data
Sedarat, Roger, 1971–
  Ghazal games : poems / Roger Sedarat.
    p. cm.
  ISBN 978-0-8214-1950-2 (pb : alk. paper) — ISBN 978-0-8214-4375-0 (electronic)
  1. Iran—Poetry. I. Title.
  PS3619.E33G43 2011
  811'.6—dc22

                        2011016090

Acknowledgments

"Ghazal Game #1": *Taj Mahal Review*

"Ghazal Game #1" (excerpt with commentary): *Pen America: A Journal for Writers and Readers*

"Sonnet Ghazal": *Literature and Gender* (New York: Pearson Longman)

"Sonnet Ghazal" and "Inverted Ghazal": *The Drunken Boat*

"Ghazal Game #2: Pin the Tail on the Middle Eastern Donkey": *Zoland Poetry*

"The Sword": *Green Mountains Review*

"American": *Rutherford Red Wheelbarrow Poets Anthology, vol. 2*

"Martyrs of Iran": *Atlanta Review: Iran Issue* and *Levantine Review*

"Postmodern Ekphrasis Ghazal": *Foreign Policy in Focus* (Poems Against the Regime)

"Protest Ghazal #1" and "Protest Ghazal #3": *IranJustice.com*

"Perfect Translation" and "Farsi": *World Literature Today*

"Cold Feet" and "Stone": *Ghazal Page*

"Gazelle in a Ghazal" and "Ghazal Game #4: Matching (Match the poet to the following couplets)": *The Other Voices International Project*

"Chador Bat, A Qasideh Ballad": *Storyscape*

"Ghazal Game #11: Spin the Bottle" and "The Beard": *New Orleans Review*

"Ghazal Game #12: Know Your Shakespeare," "Found Ghazal," and "Trapped in Form": *College English Notes*

. . . you must be ready to break the forms,
break the forms . . .

V. S. Naipaul

Contents

Ghazal Game #1

Think of the greatest love you've ever had (   ).
Write his/her name in the space provided _____.

As long as you reiterate this name,
The semblance of this ghazal is complete: _____!

Don't doubt, no matter what terror may come,
That God will fill your emptiness with Dear _____.

For me, Janette. For Dante, Beatrice.
For Rumi, Sham-y-Tabriz. And for you? _____.

Space makes the greatest rhyme. Sufis know this,
In spite of their lust for someone just like _____.

Now burn your useless books! You'll learn much more
Inside schoolhouses of desire taught by _____.

Is it so silly, making readers work?
Doesn't most poetry ask you to find _____?

"Dearly beloved, we are gathered here
To join (state your full name) and (state his/hers) _____ . . ."

Computer code, universal language,
Breaks down when translating the essence of _____.

Would you obsess over your petty shame?
Instead, substitute it with a kiss from _____.

All maps lead you to bliss. Your GPS
Just estimates the time and distance to _____.

Before the loggers come for the last tree,
Write this last line with a sharp knife: I ♥ _____.

At this point, do you think you really chose _____?
Before you were born, you were chosen by _____!

Sonnet Ghazal

for Janette

Hafez, the baker, could see what I mean;
If she were a spice, she'd be cinnamon.

It's both terrifying and exciting,
The idea that she'd see other men.

Oh, God, I'd sell my soul to watch her walk;
Hear my prayer, and grant me this sin. Amen.

I heard the great poets of Shiraz sing
Through olive vein-lines of her Persian skin.

I know; this ghazal objectifies her,
Ignoring feminist criticism.

Reversing the Cinderella story,
She turns all princes into cindermen.

"Your next patient, Doctor. It's Roger S."
"The one lovesick for his wife? Send him in."

Ghazal Game #2: Pin the Tail on the Middle Eastern Donkey

By spinning yourself you'll spin the donkey.
Sufis teach us how to pin the donkey.

At school in Cairo, we watched where we stepped.
(The groundskeeper didn't pen the donkey.)

"*Yalla, y'hmar!*" yelled at a slow driver
In an attempt to quicken the donkey.

It's all connected. One wrestles within
To change the real world and pin the donkey.

The butterflies have all been cataloged.
Hapless scientists just pin the donkey.

Can't understand this game? Stop thinking. Close
Your sense of self and open the donkey.

"Hey, poet, we're literal! We came here
With blindfolds and tacks to pin the donkey."

Let's say you hit the target. What's the point?
It's not like you really win the donkey.

A live sex act too freaky to recount
Traumatized me, the woman, the donkey . . .

If Lennon was the Walrus, I'm at best
The camel, maybe even the donkey.

Inverted Ghazal

for David Lehman

A mirror fuses false appearances;
(A mere few things in this world become one).

Amir, who drove me to Persepolis,
Insisted we speak English on the way.

A mirror used to translate a language
(i.e., dictionary) will get broken.

Ah, mirror! Who's the fairest of them all,
Since radiant Marzieh stopped singing?

A mirror: Urdu/Persian (vice/versa);
It figures Ghalib liked to read Hafez.

A Mir who married an old Khavari
Begat my great-great-grandmother Ezzat.

A mirror to a mirror back-talks twice,
Flips meaning upside down, then right again.

Am I reared rude enough in the U.S.
To violate the sacred ghazal form?

A mirrored blue sea/sky in Genesis
Revealed the first rhyme of dichotomies.

A) Mirror—2 B) God—1 C) —0.
Which of the above matches your being?

You:I, or me:Him (the eternal split
Of object and subject in poetry).

The Persian Poet's Recipe for Qormeh Sabzi

Quick! Hide this ghazal deep in your Qur'an.
(Terrorists don't understand the Qur'an.)

Would you eschew convention? Follow these
Lines to a place where truth, at its core, can

Enjamb ghazal couplets, proclaim an end
To Ramadan, and dine on the Qur'an.

Stew meat, spinach, onion, parsely, tareh,
Fenugreek, black-eyed peas, peppercorn and . . .

I know; I shouldn't be making this. Not
The food, this ghazal game of the Qur'an.

Call me Cat in the Hat or *Gorbeigh dar
Sabzi* (cat in the stew) or a whore and

A hack, subverter of sacred causes.
Sentenced to sentences in the Qur'an,

I will surrender, eat the dish I've made,
Recite the ghazal hid in the Qur'an.

(I didn't try to write it, the words came
The way the prophet transcribed the Qur'an.)

Pure agency, I arrive in Mecca
Both here and there: the world is my Qur'an.

Oh, Hallaj, your blaspheming the Qur'an
Affirms your close reading of the Qur'an.

Ghazal Game #3: True or False

(Put a "T" next to all statements that are correct and
an "F" next to those you consider false)

____ Eyes are windows. Breaking them hurts the soul.
The blindly devout monk shuttered the soul.

____ On Rita Dove's "Seven Pool Players'" graves,
This line's inscribed in blood: "We lurk the soul."

____ Not even Wall Street bonuses before
The crash could have remotely perked the soul.

____ The Trekkies' spiritual *Enterprise*
Always leads them to Captain Kirk the soul.

____ Robert Plant sang, "I don't know, but I've been
Told, a quart of malt liquor burps the soul."

____ Even the best of masturbators fail
In perverted attempts to jerk the soul.

____ Assuming an instrument could prove it,
James Brown's movements could out-berserk the soul.

____ Religion best predicts where believers,
After they die, get to insert the soul.

____ Such sins as rape, murder, and suicide
Allow the devil to usurp the soul.

____ Eliot's Prufrock proclaimed, "I grow old . . .
And my receding hairline irks the soul."

____ The symbolic can't depict the divine.
Not even "Rumi" really words the soul.

The Beard

for Marlene Clark

Now all else has failed; I'm growing my beard.
Look for the man I was behind my beard.

No Tehran taxis stop for the mullah,
Drivers spitting at each passerby's beard.

"I can't kiss you anymore," said his wife.
"It's not really you, it's . . . that ugly beard."

Excerpt from the terrorist's instructions:
"Use Clorox bleach to kill germs and dye beard."

To make the Ayatollah's effigy,
We toilet-papered a white two-ply beard.

"There's Daddy!" screamed my son, the president
Of Iran's beard the same length as my beard.

The prisoner pieced together poetry
With curlicues he plucked from his gray beard.

After the fatwa against the poet,
The CIA loaned him their best spy beard.

Dear writer of new Persian poetry,
Need an apt metonym for "man"? Try "beard."

"Hey, Khomeini!" my aunt Shirin exclaimed,
Fake-cutting my facial hair. "Good-bye beard!"

Five-letter word for overgrown shadow
Yet to be cast upon soldier boy: _____.

The poet, in the last line of "The Beard,"
When asked to state his name, just writes: "I, beard."

The Sword

It's true, "The pen's mightier than the sword."
But what cuts off the poet's hand? The sword.

Deconstructionists unscrewed handles and
Melted metal to understand the sword.

After the overthrow of the regime,
Newly elected leaders banned the sword.

Because it hurt children, as a father
I decided to reprimand the sword.

So hot in hell the holy warrior
Fed on his frozen heart and fanned the sword.

The victim's mother stopped eating kebab.
She liked the meat, but couldn't stand the sword.

Please excuse my use of "the sword." It takes
Violent language to split apart this word.

For My Beloved

I know . . . ghazals are for my beloved.
But she's been a real whore, my beloved.

Oh, baby, don't lock me out of the house.
It's cold! Open the door, my beloved.

How will we make ends meet? I lost my job
Of twenty years at Ford, my beloved.

"Dearly beloved, we gather . . ." ("It's our
Wedding, don't look so bored, my beloved.")

A literal lion lives inside me.
Your body makes him roar, my beloved.

Poor Cain. After he murdered his brother,
Abel, he could neither die nor be loved.

The world's gone bankrupt. The only wealth left
Is sold at this store: *Buy Buy Beloved.*

Devout believers point prayers to Mecca.
I direct my prayers toward my beloved.

From all the bottles of vodka I used
To drink myself dead poured my beloved.

Damn it all to hell, if only you'll bless
The greatest beauty, Lord: my beloved.

"A-B-C . . ." She turns apples' stems, breaks them
At "R," to reach my core: my beloved.

Salads Are for Girls

Clementine is right: "Salads are for girls."
Just like beauty product ads are for girls.

The show, called *Mad Men,* is about a time
When real drinking guys were madder for girls.

My whole life he couldn't hold me, much less
Offer me protection. (Dads are for girls.)

As cool as us men play it around them,
Usually our hearts shatter for girls.

"Put those down, Theo. They're Mommy's. Don't stick
Them on your brother. These pads are for girls."

Because of patriarchal pedestals,
The prince always needs a ladder for girls.

SAT analogy: "Fish are for
Chips in the UK as lads are for girls."

"Roger, don't wear Crocs and do pilates.
You've got to accept . . . these fads are for girls."

Ghazal Game #4: Matching

(Match the poet to the following couplets)

A. Rumi
B. Ghalib
C. The Poet
D. Hafez
E. Nassir Sedarat (Roger's Father)
F. You (The Reader)

1. _____ "O wise Hoopoe! To Sheba I send you.
   Understand from where to where I send you."

2. _____ "Look here, my boy, I'm wearing d'is beanie
   Because my friend got married to a Jew!"

3. _____ "Old Masters, for your gift of the ghazal
   I remain unable to repay you."

4. _____ "With greater disgrace than Adam's exile,
   I'm forced to leave the land where I met you."

5. _____ "The soul-freeing tomb may look like a jail;
   The rising sun may seem setting to you."

6. _____ "Yet another perverse ghazal from you.
   Put me in second person? It's still you!"

American

Ironically, cars, *the* American
Invention, became un-American.

In Italy, if you hear rude loudmouth
Folks speaking English, they're American.

Interestingly, these couplets' beginnings
Mess with convention (how American).

"In the beauty of the lilies, Christ was
Born across the sea" (North American).

"In Dixieland I'll take my stand, to live
And die in Dixie" (South American).

Off Brittany's coast, Lacan saw sardines
That didn't see him in a mirror can.

"Innisfree" is Irish, but the bean rows
Allude to a text that's American.

In Bugs Bunny, we meet a character
Who embodies what's most American.

"I need!" "I'm needy!!!" Personal statements
Exemplifying the American.

Necessarily, you'll need a green card
(At least) to be a free American.

In hybridity, you'll find me in the
Hyphen: Iranian (-) American.

Ghazal Game #5: Product Placement

(Name the product advertised in each couplet)

"Bam Bam!" A one-pink-bunny marching band
Across the TV. "He keeps going and . . ."

Color your magic carpet by numbers:
"(Eight hundred), five-eight-eight, two, three hundred . . ."

"I'd like to teach the world to sing, in per-
Fect harmony." (Each singer holds a hand.)

"Big Mac, Filet-O-Fish, Quarter Pounder,
French fries, icy Coke, thick shake, sundaes, and . . ."

It adds insult to injury, making
Things look easy—even for a caveman.

Burnt-out cowboy fading on the billboard
Where platform highways form an ampersand.

Cool artist type versus computer geek
Who can't compute the style some understand.

Wired from the get-go, this high-strung sailor
Feared Moby Dick. He sells hot cups on land.

Rugged American blue worn by all,
Uniquely expressing thoughts of Ayn Rand.

Martyrs of Iran

In sacred ghazals, martyrs of Iran
Die for verse. (They're all martyrs of Iran.)

The poet struck the beat upon his back;
His spiked belt buckled martyrs of Iran.

Though I pray for you, I'm far from dying.
It's impossible, martyrs of Iran.

Her name, "Neda," means voice. The whole world hears
Her silence. We're all martyrs of Iran.

Made-up American superheroes
Prove no match for real martyrs of Iran.

Killed with the Shah, my uncle's not among
True political martyrs of Iran.

Forget their sins in this transient world.
The spilled blood absolves martyrs of Iran.

Basiji kids buy toy Evin prisons
Where you torture doll-martyrs of Iran.

The thread of incense spelled Allah's ninety-
Nine names, linked to all martyrs of Iran.

One aunt shows me dark bags under her eyes,
Another wrinkles . . . (martyrs of Iran).

Outside Iran, Ali reigns among best
Worst-death Karbala martyrs of Iran.

"Dear Roger,

> *We T'ank you for this poem*
For our kids.

> *Love,*

> *All Mot'ers of Iran."*

Chemotherapy

For harm he's causing, chemotherapy
Shares guilt with his shrink (chemotherapy).

Even the atheist considered prayer
(You'll never outthink chemotherapy).

This thug, a cancer cell, walks into a bar
For his toxic drink: chemotherapy.

Dethrone the king! We're with you. The big "C"
Is a little fink, chemotherapy.

How can he be a real premed major?
His prof says he's failing Chemistry III.

"We had to burn the village to save it."
Paradoxes stink, chemotherapy.

A well-read oncologist writes poems
After prescribing chemotherapy.

Since Persians can't say "th," my bald uncle
Cried, *"For di's, I t'ank chemot'erapy."*

When their bodies recover, what helps minds
To no longer think "chemo"? Therapy?

If words were cancer, the "delete" button
Would save printer's ink, chemotherapy.

Thanks for curing me, but my eyelashes
Fall out when I blink, chemotherapy.

Vertical Ghazal

for k. bradford

```
A    D    O    M    D    L    T    M    I    O
s    o    h    a    o    i    h    a    n    f
     w    d    n'   k    e    y
i    n    E    e    t    e              A    p
f         m              r    n         d    r
     p    i    y    w    h    e    o    a,   i
f    a    l    o    o    a    a    t    m'   m
o    g    y    u    r    m    d         s    o
r    e         r    r         e    u    f    r
     s    D         y    o    r    n    a    d
t         i    n    ,    r    d    d    l    i
h    s    c    a              s    e    l    a
e    a    k    t    M    b    c    r    l    l
     n    i    u    u    a    h    s
f    s    n    r    s    c    o    t    w    l
i         s    e    l    o    o    a    e    a
r    p    o         i    o    l    n         n
s    a    n    n    m    n    e    d    s    g
t    r    ,    e    ,    ,    d         i    u
     a         w              b         n    a
t    c    r    ,    I    b    i    t    n    g
i    h    e              u    n    h    n    e
m    u    s    i    k    t    i    i    é
e    t    i    r    n         n    i    d
     e    s    o    i    h         s         (p
     e    s    n    t'   o    h    v    a    o
p    s    t    o    w    r    o    e    l    e
o         a    i         i    r    r    l    t
e    (i   n    c    i    z    t    t    :    s
t    t'   c    ,    t    o    i    i
s    s    e         f    n    c    c    a    a
          a    m    a    t    a         a    l
a    a    t    w    a    a    l    l    f    l
l    w    o    e    y    f    a         a
l    f    -    t         e         f    l    f
     u    G    f    t    l         a    l    a
f    l)   o    u    a         l    l    l    l
a         d    l    s         i         ).
l         l    t              n
l              e              e
f                             s
a
l
l
```

My Father's Face

At the end of his life my father's face
Appears in the mirror (my father's face).

Not even plastic surgery could change
The look of shame upon my father's face.

What part of people do we most recall?
Without any doubt, it's by far the face.

Though I begat my look, I've since squandered
The inheritance of my father's face.

Freud would label me the Oedipal son
Intent on erasing my father's face.

Like Christ on the cross, in my darkest hour
I cry out in vain to see my Father's face.

As if to refuse romantic cliché
Bees forgo the sweet smelly flower's face.

I can't see, in the dusty framed picture,
Any reflections of my father's face.

Since he hid behind the *Wall Street Journal,*
They undervalued his shy father's face.

It must look like most spiritually
Tough male writers: Robert Bly's father's face.

It's hard to remain faithful in a car.
You're always driving by another's face.

Despite piles of books and student essays,
I read my literary father's face.

Persian Mr. Potato Head: the nose
Of my grandma stuck on my father's face.

"Knock knock." Who's there? "Nassir." Nassir Who? "Na'
Sir, don't put a name to my father's face."

Ghazal Game #6: Hangman

(Follow directions in each couplet to draw a hangman for each missed letter)

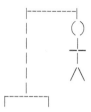

First, hang your head like Hester Prynne's letter
In shame. You belong to her sin-letter.

The lyric "I," poet, is so last year.
You're nothing more than a has-been letter.

If some nun wants to sign the cross over
Your unchristian, heathen heart, then let her.

You point out my metrical feet don't match?
Your spirit's crushed by a dead-end letter.

I get such a kick out of your power,
There's an "A"-shaped bruise on my shin, letter.

Bashō and Hafez: Japanese-Persian Fusion

for Kimiko Hahn

"The hawk's black blur through the ancient haiku . . .
Autumn afternoon." (My recent haiku.)

"Waiter, there's a moth in my noodle soup."
"Ghazal, do I taste a hint a' haiku?"

The old pond. A frog jumps. Sound of water.
(Even as one line, excellent haiku.)

I put Persian themes in Japanese form.
By "Make it new!" Ezra Pound meant haiku.

In the new century everything changed:
Books went digital; ghazals went haiku.

The Goddamn Scale

Every Friday, I hate the goddamn scale
That shows me what I ate. The goddamn scale!

"It's all that night eating you do. Don't sit
On your ass and berate the goddamn scale."

My days are numbered. I'm surrendering
To this God-awful fate: the goddamn scale.

I'm now seeing my worst fear realized:
I weigh one eighty-eight. The goddamn scale.

"Da dun ♩♩ da ♪. Hey hey hey . . . it's fa-a-a-a-a-t Roger!"
(It even *sings* my weight, the goddamn scale.)

"Wow, your husband's such a manorexic.
I bet he even dates the goddamn scale."

"Roger," says my shrink, "you're an artist. Look
For ways to recreate the goddamn scale."

The Train

Snow outlines tree branches outside the train,
The setting of a story on the train.

Where to begin? With starts and stops it's hard
To settle on a moment on the train.

"It's women!" "No, it's men!" Lacan's children
Each saw a different restroom on the train.

At home I write poetry, but I try
To write a novel when I'm on the train.

She looked just like my wife, with the same scar
Across her lips. I kissed her on the train.

I never cheat, and rarely make couplets
Cohere, but there's something about a train . . .

"I'm Persian," she said. "Me too," I replied.
This proved we really were on the same train.

"I knew we'd meet like this," she said. "But thought
Instead of snow we'd be seeing it rain."

My generation watched *Risky Business*
And recalls that great sex scene on the train.

I touched her knee. She moved my hand between
Her legs, whispering, "Take me on this train!"

"Now cut that out, you two!" the conductor
Ordered. "There are little kids on this train!"

"They're not our kids," she said, fixing her skirt.
"Who says that we can't have fun on this train?"

"The police in New Jersey! Should I call them
And say where you were headed on this train?"

Instead of sex she fixed my hair, straightened
My tie (a woman needs a man to train).

"Are you my wife," I asked, "or just some girl
I happened to connect with on the train?"

My fantasy would give me both Janette
And the wild brunette I met on the train.

Texas

Androgynous kids grow up in Texas
Hurt by the strict division of sexes.

Except for Lilas, who moved to LA,
All my exes really live in Texas.

In seventh-grade P.E., we all noticed
Bruce Dillon's schlong was the size of Texas.

My mom, who bought my clothes at garage sales,
Retired, and bought herself a new Lexus.

"We R @ the mall. Can u mt 4 lunch?
Is McD's @ 12:00 ok? Txt us."

Do men who watch online porn really cheat?
"Depends" says Bill Clinton, "on what sex is."

Mimi, my sister's daughter, makes two horns
With her fingers and hisses (her hexes).

My wife is so New York, you'd never guess
That she's from a place called Lubbock, Texas.

"Boy, in my day, before the Internet
I got my info from *LexisNexis.*"

I can't not return to my childhood state.
"You can take the poet out of Texas . . . "

Ghazal Game #7: Tic Tac Toe

(Fill in the Xs and Os where appropriate)

Strange things for Freud come in threes—"OOO,"
Like Lear's daughter's absent hugs (OOO).

I put a row of tacks at the threshold
Of my childhood room. Mom cried, "O! O! O!"

Alright, you're X; I'm O. Go! [   ][   ][   ].
But my world's predetermined: [O], [O], [O].

On *The Simpsons*, a nuclear fish swims
In Springfield with eyes like this: OOO.

God's tit for tat. For every X an O.
His grace adds up to nothing: o+o+o.

Don't read the words in Frost's "Home Burial";
Just list the "Oh's": <u>Amy</u>   <u>Man</u>
                      "Oh . . . ?"   "O,"
                      "Oh . . . !"

My first book of poetry took ten years
To write. How much did I make? $1,000.

Who here remembers *Welcome Back, Kotter*
When Horshack knew the answer, "O!, O!, O!"?

This time we'll play for real. Here: X O O.
Just like that you change the game: O [ ] O.

Is it? Could it be? Yes! A reply from
Poetry. Maybe this time . . . Nooo!!!

The ghost without form dispersed into air,
An incomprehensible b   o.
                            o

Okay, critic, you call these couplets trite?
You try making something with "OOO."

No longer blowing rings of crack smoke through
My life, God's love surrounds me: O O O.

(Re)reading Emerson's "Circles" essay
My eye expands out through space : o O O.

Well, Roger, it's getting late and readers,
They get . . . you know . . . a little tired. Sooo . . .

Postmodern Ekphrasis Ghazal

Behind typical Persian images
The artist screens CNN images.

How they pierce the Orientalist gaze,
The cut and bruised olive-skin images.

Defiant Mousavi posts "not by the
hair of my chinny chin chin" images.

Since the big crackdown, we're all wondering
What happened? Where have you *been*, images?

When I saw people die, I gave up porn
To obsess on these new sin images.

Khamenei and Khomeini for the West
Create identical twin images.

You're in cameras while bullets are in guns.
How can you possibly win, images?

My family recalls '79
And those killing of our kin images.

Ever prescient Bob Dylan foretold
Iran's new blown-in-the-wind images.

I click throughout the world for real answers,
I get this reply again: images.

Protest Ghazal #1

As outraged Iran cries, "Take back our votes!"
Khamenei denies he attacked our votes.

YouTube and Twitter: the new media.
Iran's censorship: the old black (our votes).

This time, America, stay out of it.
We hardly need you to Big Mac our votes.

Detectives dressed in green find evidence:
A dull, rusted sword used to hack our votes.

Ahmadinejad lives in poverty
Because he knows he'll always lack our votes.

Tehran tourist: keep windows up, doors locked.
Crooks are so bad here, they carjack our votes.

With rats around, I knew we shouldn't leave
Crumbs on the campaign trail to track our votes.

You wonder why this country is on fire?
See these houses? These paper shacks are votes.

Protest Ghazal #2

No movement stops these Basijis in me.
(Protests strengthen these Basijis in me.)

By claiming the hatred in his own heart
Ghandi knew well these Basijis in me.

"Hey, Ayotollah, get out of Texas!"
They speak English, these Basijis in me.

I tried cocaine, overeating, and porn:
Vain attempts to freeze Basijis in me.

I'm Persian (half at least). Can I offer
Half a glass of tea, Basijis in me?

He's lost in the forest. He cannot see
The forest through trees, Basiji in me.

My shrink says trauma opens doors to heal.
Have you seen my keys, Basiji in me?

More than the terror, guilt over mourning
Those who die fuels these Basijis in me.

The running from you and kicking through fear
Brought me to my knees, Basijis in me.

Protest Ghazal #3

Freud's case study about repressed Iran?
"Caged lion in analysis: Iran."

Exhibits in Chelsea, memoirs published . . .
You host an artistic love fest, Iran.

The truth comes out. The whole world is watching.
They cannot silence your protest, Iran.

I'm thinking of a country that censors
With thugs who wear black. Did you guess Iran?

I want to write love poetry for you,
But you burned the nightingale's nest, Iran.

Ferdowsi would have made you a court fool,
Since you don't so much reign as jest, Iran.

Will you revoke my passport for this verse?
Please do. *Befaram.* Be my guest, Iran.

They shout Allah-o-Akbar from rooftops
In hope God will restore a blessed Iran.

"Well, Roger, here's why you struggle to breathe.
X-rays show this caught in your chest: Iran."

Ghazal for Neda

All Persian poems now rhyme with Neda.
Her name in every poet's breath, "Neda."

No one believes the UK murdered you.
We know it's state-created myth, Neda.

It's not what was or what has come to pass:
We die online, in real time, with Neda.

What does the world feel for those who oppress?
"*Niente,*" "*hichchi,*" "*betsuni,*" "*niets,*" "*nada.*"

Divine symbol at your vigil: I saw
A candle flame consume a moth, Neda.

Nothing in Islam supports your murder,
Not the Qur'an, nor the Hadith, Neda.

Her name means "voice." Because she cannot sing
Iran remains in silence with Neda.

Perfect Translation

There's such a thing as "perfect translation."
It's "perfectly imperfect translation."

Bawdy poets like Martial and Iraj
Make for a kind of erect translation.

You're not a translator until you make
A good "Peter Piper picked" translation.

I gave up his verse when no press would take
My Persian Anthony Hecht translation.

I don't know why, but it hurts just as much
When the top journals reject translation.

Shias and Sunnis use the same Qu'ran,
Avoiding two different sect translations.

What do you get when you cross Whitman with
Latino verse? Electric translation.

"Not that verb, Henry! Use this word." His wife
Made him render such henpecked translation.

George Babel, famous linguist, invented
A program that can detect translation.

In the new world, the Geneva Bible
Became the "divine elect" translation.

"It's Hafez, Roger. You set yourself up
In English when you expect translation."

Cold Feet

Watch out where she steps or you'll touch cold feet.
(She broke my meter with her crutch-cold feet.)

Straight out single step if it's been a while;
Don't just jump in and double-dutch cold feet.

Autumn mornings the children march on grapes,
Hence this remark from the wine judge: "Cold feet!"

Good doctors, to prevent diabetic
Amputations, inspect bluish old feet.

A metric program insures your lines scan,
But I'd prefer free verse to such cold feet.

The Emperor of Ice Cream fetishized
Fabric on corpses' butterscotch-cold feet.

Of course I want to marry the divine.
It's not a refusal; it's just cold feet.

Ghazal Game #8: An Exercise in Tone

(Read the following couplets with relevant tone for the subject matter)

Where have you been? It's about fucking time
I scream out loud, "It's about fucking time!"

Hair loss, weight gain, and wrinkles. Older folks
Understand what it's about: fucking time.

After failed interventions, the U.S.
Brought home the troops. It's about fucking time.

The story of sabotage throws wrenches
In old Big Ben (it's about fucking time).

Porn stars consider how long they can go
The real measure: It's about fucking time.

The older LA woman, nipped and tucked,
Flashed her plastic tits about, fucking time.

The barbershop had *S.I.* (it's a-
Bout sports), *Hustler* (it's about fucking), *Time* . . .

"Tick! Come on baby! Now tock! Tock for me!"
Oh, don't mind that; it's Bob, out fucking time.

Have you guys seen the new postmodern play
Fast Clocks, Hard Cocks? It's about fucking time.

You don't understand *Mrs. Dalloway?*
Give me a break, it's about fucking time.

"Damn Roger, at last you end this stupid
Naughty poem. It's about fucking time!"

Facebook

An online album of friends on Facebook.
Why go to parties? Stay in on Facebook.

"Kids finally asleep. Mojito time!"
(Lara, my fifth-grade girlfriend on Facebook.)

I never, as a rule, talk politics
Or show off my kids, but when on Facebook . . .

You age well here: it's easy to save face
And you don't have to weigh-in on Facebook.

Some protesters in Iran have vanished.
I last saw these long-lost friends on Facebook.

Though my wife and I always work at home,
It's hard to poke her (even on Facebook).

People don't really look how they appear.
Plato's *Republic* would frown on Facebook.

My profile lists me as Muslim and Jew
To model coexistence on Facebook.

She calls herself Emily Dickinson,
This hot Egyptian woman on Facebook.

Call for poems: "Found Poetry from Friends'
New updates: A Collection on Facebook."

It's not a competition, but I have
A couple hundred more friends on Facebook.

To get to know cultural artifacts
Of our time, "friend" the iPhone on Facebook.

"Welcome to the worst time suck of your life."
My first greeting from a friend on Facebook.

"Roger's writing couplets about posting
Thoughts about the postmodern on Facebook."

Ghazal Game #9: Illustrate the Comic Strip

(Follow the couplet captions, The Burbs, about a couple who moved from Manhattan to the New Jersey suburbs, to draw the appropriate picture)

1. "I know we've just unpacked in the suburbs,
    But how long must we live in the suburbs?"

2. "So now we're driving to New York City
    Because you can't give birth in the suburbs?"

3. "We're in Venice, for Christsakes, why convince
    Gondoliers we don't live in the suburbs?"

4. "It's a group influenced by the Supremes
    Comprised of three WASP women: "The Superbs.""

5. (This Bogart-type at a soccer practice):
   "What's a dame like you do in the suburbs?"

6. "I made him clean his dog's poop from my yard.
   That's how we roll out here in the suburbs."

7. "It *is* a poem (based on a comic
   Based on our tragic life in the suburbs)."

8. "But the neighbor boy can't be our doorman.
   We live in a house now . . . in the suburbs!"

9. "Don't mow a sad face in the lawn, Roger.
   They're much less ironic in the suburbs."

Gazelle in a Ghazal

for G. C. Waldrep

Named after the gazelle's cry, "the ghazal"
Imprisoned gazelles via the ghazal.

Rhymes reproduce connections, aural mir-
Rors: mimetic fallacy / the ghazal.

My father cried his life was all a lie,
"Same old material," sighed the ghazal.

As the lion will stalk prey, the poet
Plans to self-identify the ghazal.

Traditions endure; in a postmodern
Age, there are Persians who write the ghazal.

One word recurs at the end of my life
Like each couplet's ending by the ghazal.

Resisting the couplet's will to define
Reorders (unconsciously) the ghazal.

It goes without saying, but he who lives
By the ghazal will die by the ghazal.

Art will be known for style more than for theme.
In Ghalib we recognize the ghazal.

Know that I love you in my refusal
To use my love to inscribe the ghazal.

The court once funded the form. Now poets
Workshop to teach and delight the ghazal.

In case it matters, I'll tell you: my name
Is Haji; I live inside the ghazal.

Ya Baba

(An imitation from the Arabic of a popular song celebrating the life of a spiritual man from Tunisia)

for Rajiv Mohabir

Before I read the refrain, "Ya baba!"
I need everyone to scream, "Ya baba!"

"I'll come to you, great master, with candles
For your everlasting beam, ya baba!"

It literally means "Oh my father."
"Wow, Dad, a new car. For me? Ya baba!"

I awoke to a wife and two children
Like from a Genesis dream. Ya baba!

A million kind acts through the Middle East
Get ignored by blind news teams. Ya baba!

Fred Flintstone's 5 o'clock "Yaba Daba
Dooo!" best states the joyous theme. Ya baba!

Somewhere, someone's immersed in Whitman's verse,
Hearing America sing. Ya baba!

"How'd you manage to survive your childhood?"
Asked the incredulous shrink. Ya baba!

"Where did he take my heart, the black-eyed one
With beautiful vibrant cheeks? Ya baba!"

After harsh words, my wife and I made love,
Letting off weeks worth of steam. Ya baba!

You were a child charging into the arms
Of your father or mother. Ya baba!

My close friend R—a radiant beauty,
Survives breast cancer (stage three). Ya baba!

One day the U.S. comes to its senses
And brings home all its army. Ya baba.

We can't work out the math, but when aware,
We sense the world's just a dream. Ya baba!

I'm going to start drumming and singing words.
At each second line's end scream, "Ya baba!"

Let's clap too. We're cheering for the divine.
I'll go elsewhere. You repeat, "Ya baba."

Sidi Mansour (ya baba), we recite
Your name in God's great rhyme scheme, ya baba.

One poet has power; our collective
Chant channels radiant beams. Ya baba.

Don't worry about outcomes, says Rumi,
Just keep fishing in God's stream. Ya baba.

Your fate, like clothes you wear, has been pre-stitched
Yet you long to see the seam. Ya baba.

Express the love of language with the tip
Of the tongue, the lips, and teeth. Ya baba.

Sins of a belly dance in the alley
Of Tunis are now redeemed. Ya baba.

We sought style over meaning, found cosmic
Spirit in figures of speech. Ya baba.

I kissed the master's feet and asked him how
To overcome so much shame, ya baba.

"Help us resist the evil that appears.
Oh God, lead our witnessing! Ya baba!"

Stop chanting now, but in your heart and mind,
Keep hearing these words repeat, "ya baba . . ."

Especially in silence the presence
Of Sidi Mansour's perceived. Ya baba.

What happened to the poet called Roger?
He's been claimed by divine peace. Ya baba!

Dubai

Despite all the bombs of George W.
Arabs build on the image of Dubai.

"Doobie doobie doo." Strangers in the night
Trade glances at the exchange of Dubai.

New York took its goods but reserved the right
Not to sell its port (the Grinch of Dubai).

"It's just a western construct based on oil."
Oh, hush! Who are you . . . the judge of Dubai?

If Iran bans his poetry, smugglers
Will sneak it through a passage of Dubai.

Who cares about Paris or New York when
We're now living in the age of Dubai?

I shall arise and go now, and go to
Steal new cars from a garage of Dubai.

Be a materialistic Muslim:
Skip Mecca and make a Haj of Dubai.

A Baudrillardian doppleganger:
Glass walls reflect the image of Dubai.

New U.S. for the Mideast, immigrants
Risk leaving home for the wage of Dubai.

In trying times sheiks count billions instead
Of trillions (the penny pinch of Dubai)

Poor Haji, too broke to afford Dubai
He sits and romanticizes Dubai.

Few play ghazal games in America,
But we hear it's all the rage of Dubai.

Dramatic Crime Scene Ghazal

for Luis Muñoz & Richard Schotter

Characters
    Don—Fat white cop in suburban New Jersey
    Joe—Don's partner (just joined force in New Jersey)
    Jamal—Arab American physics teacher
    Leila—Jamal's wife (law student in New Jersey)

Don: "Freeze, punk! What have we here? Oh, it's your vial
        Filled up with snow. Been skiing somewhere? Vail?"

Jamal: "You planted that! I don't do drugs. Is it
        Because I'm Arab? Damn, you cops are vile."

Don: "Shut up, you terrorist. Joe, search his wife
        All over. Find out what's under her veil."

Leila: "If you touch me, you're going to lose your badge.
        Think about it: this is a lawyer's veil."

Joe: (Don starts to clutch his chest.) "Don! You okay?"

Don: "It's heartburn . . . probably from that rare veal."

Jamal: "It's divine justice. Like in that movie
        Crash. God's punishing you for your evil."

Don: "Nah, sand nigger. I'll take a couple Tums
        Then give it to your wife under her veil."

Don: (Begins to stroke Leila's exposed dark hair.)
        "Honey, you feel so good under your veil."

Leila: "Perpetrator! You don't have a warrant!
        I'll prosecute you! The law will prevail!"

        (Don falls to the ground. When EMTs come
        He's covered with a sheet [another veil].)

                    Curtain
                    (Curtain)

Ghazal Game #10: Truth or Dare

Here's your chance. Risk your life. Choose truth or dare.
Do it now! Snooze and you lose truth or dare.

It's hard to play with Buddhists. They collapse
All binaries and fuse truth or dare.

In your longest-term sex relationship,
Did you fake your moans and coos? Truth or dare?

Mention your last crime or go tell wise guys,
"I don't like the look of *youse.*" Truth or dare.

If you could have someone else's sex life,
Confess to your partner whose. Truth or dare.

(I know; this one's lame): What's the most you've owed
In unpaid library dues? Truth or dare?

These all seemed designed by men to enjoy
Women's desires. Tell us: *whose* truth or dare?

Did you, even once, think about giving
Your over-wired toddler booze? Truth or dare.

All right, Roger, since you designed this game,
Pick a couplet here and choose: truth or dare?

Moley

His brunette wife's thin and pretty moley.
I saw her changing clothes. (Holy moley!)

Hafez would trade Tamerlane's Samarkand
For the size of this Shirazi mole: "**e.**"

A restaurant in West San Antonio
Brings the best chips with free guacamole.

Spies pose as diplomats inside Iran;
A good disguise (bureaucracy's moley).

"Single man seeking Persian woman. Must
Love basement jazz. Preferred she be moley."

Accept the good with the bad: drench the whole
Enchilada in bittersweet mole.

"I'll get this one removed!" exclaims my wife.
"Divorce!" I yell. "You married me moley!"

Farsi

In English you say "Persian," not "Farsi."
(My eighth-grade English teacher taught Farsi.)

Arabs couldn't pronounce the "P" in "Pars."
Persians should say it "Parsi," not "Farsi."

Trope of letters for a bird on a wave
In English looks like "bird/wave: dot/Farsi."

American tourist ad for Iran:
Persian woman licking lips: "Got Farsi?"

My Persian sucks. In translation, I sound
Like this: "Me not speaking a lot Farsi."

"I took this Persian girl back home last night.
She whispered in my ear some hot Farsi."

"Roger, please don't mock my cousins' fighting.
It's called family *drama*, not *farce*, see?"

Chador Bat, a Qasideh Ballad

It just turned spring. This poem, "Chador Bat,"
A baharieh, must first mention that.

I didn't want to work in the orchard
With cousin Shirin (she called my mom fat).

"A-choo." I faked terrible allergies
(Dramatic culture taught me how to act).

"Stay home, *Haji-jan*," said my grandma Taj;
"We'll water the norangis and come back."

I raced through the house in my aunt's chador,
A child of the night out on the attack.

A Persian qasideh ought to diverge
Midway through its theme: This poem does that.

It first doubts the verisimilitude,
Questions of figurations versus fact.

It then critiques the Orientalist
Perspective of what this poet looks at.

Biography follows, significance
Of this poet named Roger Sedarat.

Reductive scholarship begins to kill
The preteen spirit of the chadored bat.

So I again fly around my aunts' house,
Escaping stupid postmodern chitchat.

Thus, the qasideh returns to its theme
As it recreates tension in climax.

I stood upon her vanity to stare
Into the mirror. "Look, I'm Aunt Bejat."

Open-shut. First man, then woman. How free
In spring to find I could be this or that.

Dichotomous mystery. And God said,
"Let the mouse be juxtaposed with the cat."

Language inevitably slips and veils
The meaning behind names like "Aunt Bejat."

The truth is she was on her way back home
Like the kid's mom in *The Cat in the Hat.*

I didn't know. I was having a ball
In her room, swinging my dick like a bat.

"Sheitune!" she screamed (calling me devil).
"Haji-jan, tell me, why would you do that?"

The truth is I had no real idea.
It hurt to see my aunt so shocked and sad.

I quickly hid my nakedness in shame
With my uncle Hajdayee's World Cup hat.

I walked away backwards, stepping over
Her chador on the ground like a dead bat.

Ghazal Game #11: Spin the Bottle

I need a kiss, so I spin the bottle.
(Desire is contained within the bottle.)

His father's getting punished on Earth for
The ultimate Muslim sin: the bottle.

Ever notice how it stops on cousins?
It's most attracted to kin, the bottle.

When this line stops, you have to kiss the next
Man or woman who walks in. l--------/ >
                                                          l----------/.

The homeless carny said, "Toss this ring on
This beer bottle, and you'll win the bottle."

Monogamous marriage means two people
Eternally have to spin the bottle.

Yo', here's the master street-life diet plan.
Guess what you can have for din? The bottle.

We flicked the bottle to move the goldfish,
Then we watched the goldfish fin the bottle.

Technology killed the childlike wonder
Over how the ship got in the bottle.

Who can forget the Police's "SOS";
It's incessant "message in a bottle"?

Dear Roger S.,

      How is sobriety?
(I've missed you.) Where have you been?

      —The Bottle

Gus

Gus drinks a lot. They call him "glug glug Gus."
His wife begs, "Put the plug in the jug, Gus."

if e.e. cummings had gone to iran
his verse would've cut a persian rug gas.

Burn your soul from thinking you're God? Most docs
In the U.S. prescribe *Atlas Shrugged Gauze.*

"So he just starts talking to his bare feet.
We were all like, 'Hey, you okay? Uh . . . Gus?'"

Critic of the poet is "Sam the Owl,"
Aghast at light-words of the firefly, Gus.

O peddlers of such shitty crafts, the mall
Is bad enough to walk through. Don't bug us!

It's Persian candy. I stopped eating it
Because my cavities really dug *gaz.*

"Shoot me up? I've been filled with so much lead,
I take Scantron tests . . . I'm one sharp fuck, cuz."

He writes so dirty, his own Persian mom
Swatted him and called him a fly (*magas*).

Real Catholics refer to "St. Augustine."
Unitarians relax among "Gus."

Richard Poirier's book compelled me toward Frost;
I didn't have to meet him at Rutgers.

We poets work hard and get rejected.
Readers, buy our books, or at least hug us.

Good God, Gus! Good gravy! You did it now.
An ass-backwards move. They call you "suG," Gus.

Let it be mentioned at his funeral
That he enjoyed junk food and liked to cuss.

Gus goes to Washington. Gus lobbies for
His own cause: tax breaks for an agog Gus.

We

Close thumb and pinkie, a "W-E."
Flick wrist and spell sassy *"whateva"* (we).

Muhammad Ali became his public,
Rhyming "Me" with adoring masses: "We."

Est-il possible écrire un couplet
Ghazal en français entre l'anglais? Oui.

We won the football game! "Dun dun dun, da
Dun, dun dun dun, da dun, Louie Louie . . ."

An introduction to Persian grammar:
man: I; *to:* you; *u:* he; she, it; *ma:* we.

It removes the drunk from isolation,
The first word of step one in AA: "We."

"Where did we go wrong with our older son?"
"I know you're blaming. You can drop the 'we'!"

Go on and cry little piggy. That's right.
Go and cry to your mama: "Wee, wee, wee!"

"Can *we* sharpen our pencil?" (White privileged
Suburban teachers use the royal "we.")

With seconds left in double overtime,
My son says, "Daddy, I gotta wee wee!"

The classical masters followed rhyme schemes
And troped their names in last couplets. May we?

Ghazal Game #12: Know Your Shakespeare

(Guess the play from which each couplet quotes)

Question: better "to be or not to be?"
Advice: " . . . a borrower nor lender be."

Monolingual audiences can grasp,
"but, for mine own part it was Greek to me."

Here's a good one for my pothead students:
"I wasted time, and now doth time waste me."

An argument of land and sea service:
"I will praise any man that will praise me."

"The most peaceable way [to] take a thief,
is, to let him . . . steal out of your company . . ."

The history of all relationships
Deftly reported: "What must be shall be."

At this point I'm giving away answers.
Here: "O! Beware, my lord, of jealousy."

Eponymous questioner who asks, "Is
This a dagger which I see before me?"

In this play, adversaries in law try
To remain friends as they "strive mightily."

Was it so good to be the king? He cried,
"The little dogs and all . . . they bark at me."

This last one's hard, and sums up my whole life:
"A man I am, cross'd with adversity."

Stone

Most people end up with a heart of stone,
Except sculptors who learn the art of stone.

Every morning I shop for family meals,
Pushing, like Sisyphus, my cart of stone.

Michelangelo's David is perfect,
But, like most men, he has a heart of stone.

All that's left of alabaster flowers
I once gave her is this red shard of stone.

Lot's wife, who lusted for one quick look back,
Got what she had coming (that tart of stone!).

Pink Floyd sang, "Shine on you crazy diamond."
Rock makes precocious kids a part of stone.

I hear they cut limbs off beggar kids. Still,
I give change. I don't have a heart of stone.

The town of Springfield should build "Mount Simpsons":
A "Marge," "Homer," "Lisa," and "Bart" of stone.

"Shoppers, Roger's soul's on sale in aisle 4."
Is there anything Walmart doesn't own?

Mixed Metaphor

for John Weir

A Gemini, I'm a mixed metaphor,
Both a strong and a henpecked metaphor.

Bashō's images are the things they are;
His melon is no mud-flecked metaphor.

The hyper-real postmodern age mirrored
Our lives. It killed art and wrecked metaphor.

New software scanned couplets of this poem;
It suggested rhymes and checked metaphor.

Those drivers turning their heads toward the crash
Extend clichéd rubberneck metaphor.

His reading of post-structural theory
Explains the poet's Žižeked metaphor.

Jonathan Edwards used the web to catch
Sinners (a divine elect metaphor).

Look, here's the actor's hand holding a pen
To play the writer, a Brecht metaphor.

Found Ghazal

(New York Subway) "If you see something,
                 Say something."

(Poet's talk with his son) "You hungry?" "Yeah."
"What do you want to eat?" "Something."

(Poet's wife after work) "I'm one fried banana.
I also think I'm coming down with something."

(Beatles song) "Something in the way she moves at-
tracts me like no other lover. Something . . ."

(U.K.answers.yahoo.com)
"In an essay, when do I quote something?"

(Robert Frost poem about looking in
water well) Title: "For Once, Then, Something."

(Poet's mom in adolescence) "Roger,
What's wrong with your eyes? Are you *on* something?"

Disease of Self

The world's infected. A disease of self.
O divine love, grant us release of self.

Create a greater whole (community)
By daily giving up a piece of self.

She didn't really want enlightenment,
Her soul subjected to the tease of self.

A legalistic maverick, within
Me lie so many Khomeinis of self.

At the bare minimum, serve each other
As co-workers, fire the big cheese of self.

Around the thorny rose of all desires,
The piercing buzz from killer bees of self.

Outside approval, awards, and money
Become mere fleeting victories of self.

I'm somewhere folded between my childhood
And future, wrinkling this faint crease of self.

Vampire God

for Nicole Cooley

Yours gives? Mine's what they call a vampire god.
My blood? He drinks it all, the vampire god.

He sleeps during the day. Sneak in his house,
Pack his things, and U-haul the vampire god.

No cross idolizes his suffering;
Victims' neck holes symbol the vampire god.

Junkies are faithful to their religion;
They'll die if you withdraw the vampire god.

True Blood, on HBO, is pulp fiction
To die for. Alan Ball's a vampire god.

Graffiti trick: draw fangs on Dick Cheney
With U.S. blood. Ta-da! A vampire god.

"Cigarettes don't cause cancer. You can smoke
An unfiltered Pall Mall."
                                        —the vampire god

Orthodox Jews, once bitten, follow him
By Talmudic law: the vampire G-d.

"The same life-bleeding routine every night.
We need a change. It's so . . . *blah,* vampire god."

Found on the men's room wall: "Need a hard suck
That will change your life? Call the vampire god."

I know he's cold, and family's dead to him.
He's hardly a "Shangri La" vampire god.

Don't judge me for being so self-seeking.
I'm just a servant: fault the vampire god.

Trapped in Form

In an age of free verse I'm trapped in form.
I'd explain it more, but I'm trapped in form.

How fitting to bury ghazal-writing
Poets in starched white sheets, gift-wrapped in form.

I teach Notorious BIG songs
To show how brilliantly he rapped in form.

While watching Michael Phelps, I wrote couplets,
An uncanny connection: lapped in form.

Stevens says poets don't choose their poems.
Frost proves his theory, as he's apt in form.

The marine sergeant was such a tight ass,
There were rumors he even crapped in form.

I lead my students through so much metered
Poetry they've nicknamed me "Captain Form."

Jar in Shiraz

for George Held

Stevens never placed a jar in Shiraz.
Voilà! I'm placing a jar in Shiraz.

After they took the poets from their homes,
The goons left all doors ajar in Shiraz.

I have an uncle descended from kings.
Here's his memoir: *A Qajar in Shiraz.*

Too long with my wife's Persian family,
I turn into a badger in Shiraz.

Hey Mario, no pasta! Eat rice, eh?
This not'a our Roma . . . ch'ur in Shiraz!

You stole in the village!!! Do you know what
The legal system of Sharia is?

It's how you say a thing. You should know that
By now about me, "Rah-jar" in Shiraz.

Sedarat

"He's *not* Haji! He's Roger Sedarat!
He made up his Persian name," said a rat.

"Tuck in that shirt when salting fries! Take pride
In that Wendy's uniform, Sedarat."

My dad thought "Roger Ted" would keep me safe,
Offsetting the foreign harm: Sedarat.

"Dare Ed to eat a rat." One of several
Phrases that can be made from "Sedarat."

I kick ass at Nerf basketball. "Down two
In O.T. . . . It's a 3 . . . Bam! Sedarat!"

"It's not you, Roger. It's patriarchy.
I won't be forced to say I'm 'Sedarat.'"

"He's not rich; he's the son of two teachers.
That bank's just a homonym: *Saderat.*"

Potato-potato, America:
You ask "Sederit?" I scream, "Sedarat!"

What's in a name? Three vowels, four consonants,
Dysfunction, and lots of shame: Sedarat.

I grew up dropping the ball, dragged through mud,
Blackening my jersey name, "Sedarat."

After his divorce, my dad called himself
Roger, like we were the same Sedarat.

At two years old I ate alphabet soup.
My mom says I pooped my name: "**S-E-D-A-R-A-T**."